Martin Luther

Martin Luther was born on the 10th of November, 1483. He was ordained a priest at the age of twenty-four. Later he was appointed to a life-long position as professor of theology at Wittenberg, Germany, where he translated the Bible into the German language.

Luther's role in the history of music was also significant; his hymns opened a new era in music. He is best known for **A Mighty Fortress Is Our God,** and he is also responsible for the Christmas song, **Away In A Manger.**

Cover Photo: The Wandering Eternal Jew 1852.

Reprinted 2004 by
Liberty Bell Publications
PO Box 890
York, SC 29745
www.libertybellpublications.com
803.684.4408

ISBN:1-59364-024-2

Printed in the United States of America

INTRODUCTION

In preparing to read this book you are about to view some of the most sensational and thought arresting language ever to be put into print.

The publishers of this treatise by Dr. Martin Luther, the pioneer of Protestantism, do not necessarily present this work as an accurate expression of their opinion. The chief reason for its publication is to give the reader an accurate translation of Luther's treatment of one of the most delicate and dangerous subjects for a public man to discuss-- the Jews.

This translation is not presented as a sectarian work or a partisan treatise. When we set out to find the book in its original language and when we proceeded to have it translated, we were shocked and amazed at the interference we encountered from a wide variety of sources. Two different translators were made the victims of intimidation, and only after a rather dramatic experience were we able to complete its translation in spite of its brevity.

In effecting the translation of this work we became increasingly convinced that a well organized plot to keep this book hidden exists.

Luther's experience with the Jews was very disappointing. He spent many years trying to convert them. Like St. Paul, he gave the Jews the first chance at the gospel, but concluded in later years, as the reader will soon see, that his efforts in this direction were futile.

This book is published only in the interest of accuracy. If it falls into the hands of a highly technical student of the 16th Century German, the Publishers will appreciate any correction which might improve the next edition of this work. The demand for this little book is so great that we expect it to go into numerous editions. We find among sincere Christian people a deep resentment over the fact that the work of one as prominent as Martin Luther has been kept so scientifically and so deliberately away from the eyes of his millions of admirers.

Some of Dr. Luther's language will shock the reader, but it is our business to give you the words of the Reformer just as he wrote them, and not on the basis of our agreement or disagreement.

Regardless of any other purpose that this translation may serve, it will serve one fundamental purpose; namely, this generation is not the first generation which has faced a Jewish problem. Yes, it will serve a second purpose; namely, an alertness to the Jewish problem does not necessarily indicate that the individuals who are alerted are depraved or un-Christian.

The Publishers.

Note: The readers of this work are warned

4

not to conclude that the Luther viewpoint concerning the Jews is necessarily Protestant. Numerous Popes used language as strong, if not stronger, than the language used by Dr. Luther. In fact, the ghettos were established by Papal edict, and the segregation of Christian communities from Jewish communities originated in edicts coming out of Rome. The purpose of this note is to warn the readers that the problem has never been uniquely Protestant or Catholic or in any way sectarian. Men of all faiths have agreed with Luther and men of all faiths have disagreed with Luther.

Attention, Doubters: Some individuals will doubt that these writings originated with Martin Luther. For the information of the reader the original language may be found in Martin Luther's works in the Congressional Library, Washington, D.C., and in any one of several accredited Lutheran seminaries. Numerous clergymen of all denominations are aware of the existence of this work. They are also aware of the fact that this is the first English translation to be published in the United States —so far as we are able to ascertain.

Note: This published work by Luther was among the last of his writings. Luther, it will be recalled, died in the prime of life, having lived only to the age of 63.

THE JEWS
AND
THEIR LIES

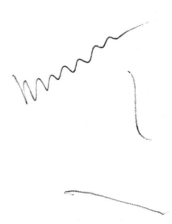

I had decided not to write anymore, neither of the Jews, nor against the Jews. Because I have learned, however that those miserable, wicked people do not cease trying to win over to themselves us, that is, the Christians also, I have permitted this booklet to go forth that I might be found among those who have resisted such poisonous undertaking of the Jews, and have warned the Christians to be on their guard against them. I would not have thought that a Christian would permit himself to be fooled by the Jews to share their exile and misery. But the Devil is the God of the world, and where God's word is not, he has easy sailing, not only among the weak, but also among the strong. God help us. Amen.

MARTIN LUTHER.

Grace and Peace in the Lord!

Dear Sir and Good Friend:

I have received a treatise of a Jew carrying on a conversation with a Christian in which the Jew has the audacity to pervert and misconstrue the passages of Scripture (which we use for our faith, of our Lord Christ, and of Mary, His mother) whereby he means to overthrow the foundation of our faith.

To this I give to you and to him this answer. It is not my intention to quarrel with the Jews or to learn from them how they interpret and understand the Scriptures. I have known all that before. Much less do I intend to convert the Jews. For that is impossible. Nor does it do any good among the Jews everywhere, and they have generally become worse. Also, because they became so hardened to visitations that they do not want to become conscious of the terrible dilemma, that they have now been in exile for over fourteen hundred years, and cannot yet see an end or a definite time (of relief) through fervent, eternal crying and screaming to God (as they suppose). (I say) If visitations do not help, we might as well figure that our talking and interpreting will help much less.

NO USE TO QUARREL

Therefore a Christian should be satisfied and not quarrel with the Jews. But if you think you must or desire to talk with them, do not say more than this: "Do you hear, Jew, do you know that your principality together with the temple and priesthood are destroyed now for 1460 years? For this year, as we Christians write after the birth of Christ 1543, it is exactly 1469 years, and is thus going on 1500 years since Vespasianus and Titus destroyed Jerusalem and expelled the Jews from it." On this little nut let the Jews bite and dispute among themselves as long as they want to.

For such terrible wrath of God is sufficient proof that they certainly must be in error and doing wrong; even a child can grasp that. For no one should think of God so terrible that He would punish his own nation so unmercifully and keep silent by neither comforting words nor indicating the duration or end of such misery! Who would want to believe in such a God, hope in Him, or trust in Him? Therefore, this wrath leads to the conclusion that the Jews are certainly rejected by God and are not His people anymore, and He also is not their God anymore; according to the passage, Hosea 1:9 *"Lo, Ammi: You are not my people, so also am I not your God."* Yea, they are in a terrible dilemma. Whatever interpretation they may place on it, we see the thing before our eyes, it does not deceive us.

VICTIMS OF THE WRATH OF GOD

And wherever there should be a spark of sense and reason in them, they would certainly think to themselves thus: "O Lord God, things are not right with us, our misery is too great, our exile too long and too hard, God has forgotten us," etc. I, of course, am not a Jew, but I seriously do not like to think about such terrible wrath of God over this nation. I shudder so much that it penetrates my body and life. What will be the eternal wrath of God in hell over all false Christians and unbelievers?

Well, the Jews may regard our Lord Jesus Christ as whatever they desire; we see the fulfillment of Luke 21:20-23: *"When ye shall see Jerusalem compassed with armies, then know that the desolation thereof is nigh-- for these be the days of vengeance, that all things which are written may be fulfilled."* [King James Version, Chapter 21:20, 22].

In short, as was said: Do not dispute much with the Jews about the articles of our faith. From childhood they have been brought up with poison and hatred against our Lord, that there is no hope until they arrive at the point where through their misery they become soft and compelled to confess that the Messiah has come and is our Lord Jesus Christ. Otherwise it is altogether too soon, yea, altogether in vain to dispute with them...In order to strengthen our faith, we shall consider a few instances of foolishness in their faith and interpretation of the Scriptures, because they slander our faith in such a mean way. Should it bring about the improvement of a Jew, that he become ashamed, so much the better! We are not talking *with* the Jews, but *of* the Jews and their deeds, which our German people well know.

They hold one principle on which they depend and in which they trust so much. That is, they are born of the highest people on earth, of Abraham, Sarah, Isaac, Rebecca, Jacob, etc. We (Goyim) heathen are not human beings in their sight, but hardly worthy to be regarded as worms. For we are not of that high, noble blood, birth and descent.

This is their argument, and in my opinion the foremost and strongest. Therefore, God must suffer them in their schools, prayers, songs, doctrine and entire life; there they stand before Him and pester Him (that I may speak of God in such human manner). He must hear how they exalt themselves and praise God for separating them from the heathen, and permitting them to be born of the holy fathers and chosen them for His own, holy nation, etc. And there is no end of boasting about blood and bodily birth of the fathers.

THEIR SELF-RIGHTEOUS BOASTING

In order that their raving, frantic and foolish nonsense might be perfect, they praise and thank God, *first*, that they are human beings and not animals; *secondly*, that they are Israelites and not Goyim (heathen); *thirdly*, that they were created as *Men* and not as *Women*. Such foolishness they do not have from Israel, but from the Goyim. For thus the historians write that the Greek Plato daily gave such praise and thanks to God, if such blasphemy and haughtiness could be called the praise of God. For that man also praised his gods for these three things, that he was man and not animal, a man and not a woman, a Greek and not a non-Greek of barbarus. Such is the praying of a fool and the praise of a blasphemous barbarus; just as the Mals imagine that they alone are human beings and all the rest of the world nothing but inhuman beings, ducks, or mice.

Well, no one can deprive them of their boasting about blood and the tribe of Israel. In the Old Testament they lost many a battle on that account. (No Jew understands this.) All prophets have chided them because of it, for it is a proud, carnal assumption without spirit and faith; but they have also been murdered and persecuted because of it.

CHILDREN OF THE DEVIL

Our Lord also calls them *"Vipers"* In John 8:39: *"If ye were Abraham's children, ye would do the works of Abraham."* Verse 44: *"Ye are of your father, the Devil."*

This was unbearable for them, that they should be the children of the Devil, as they cannot bear it yet. For if they would have to give us this foundation (Abraham's children), everything they have built upon it would have to fall and be different. [In the following this self-praise is refuted from Scripture as unfounded assumptions. These dissertations then close with these words:] But this will I say for the strengthening of our faith. For the Jews will not let this pride and this glory of their nobility and blood be taken away from them, as said above. They are hardened.

Our people, however, should be on their guard against these hardened, condemned people (who accuse God of lying and proudly despise the whole world), that they be not misled. For the Jews would gladly entice us to accept their faith and do so wherever they can. For if God should be gracious toward the Jews, they first would have to do away out of their schools, out of their hearts, and out of their mouths, all such blasphemous prayers and songs, and the boasting and pride about their blood. For such prayer constantly increases God's wrath upon them. But they will not do this, nur humble themselves, except a few individuals whom God draws especially and redeems them from their terrible destruction.

EXALT THEMSELVES

The other boast and superiority, on account of which they exalt themselves above all other people and despise them, is this: that from Abraham on down they have *circumcision*. God help, how we heathen here must suffer in their schools, prayers, songs and teaching! How ugly we despised people stink before their noses because we are not circumcised, etc. ..

[Here follow lengthy theological treatises based on numerous passages from Scripture.] They are pictured in it in a masterful manner before all heathen; for they are the very people who always practiced such ungodly manner of idolatry, and false doctrine, and have had uncircumcised hearts as Moses himself, and all prophets lament over them; but at the same time have endeavored to please God and for that reason killed the prophets. They are the wicked and hardened people who did not suffer themselves to be converted from their evil to good deeds through preaching, teaching, chiding of the prophets, as Scripture testifies everywhere. Yet they want to be God's servants and stand before Him! They are boastful, proud fools who to this day can not do more than to praise themselves because of their nobility and blood; praise themselves alone and despise and condemn the whole world in their schools, prayers, and teachings; yet they imagine themselves to be standing before God as His dearest children!

LIARS AND BLOODHOUNDS

They are the real liars and bloodhounds, who have not only perverted and falsified the entire Scriptures from beginning to end and without ceasing with their interpretations. And all of the anxious sighing, longing and hope of their hearts is directed to the time when some day they would like to deal with us heathen as they dealt with the heathen in Persia at the time of Esther...O how they love that book Esther, which so nicely agrees with their bloodthirsty, revengeful and murderous desire and hope! The sun never did shine on a more bloodthirsty and revengeful people as they who imagine to be the people of God who desire to and think they must murder and crush the heathen. And the foremost undertaking which they expect of their Messiah is that He should slay and murder the whole world with their sword. As they at first demonstrated against us Christians and would like to do do so now, if they only could; have also tried it often and have been repeatedly struck on their snouts. But of this perhaps later.

[Here Luther uncovers the deepest cause of the ever-recurring persecution of the Jews: their own fault and overbearing pride. Luther now enumerates more references of which the Jews boast, in addition to circumcision; the Mosaic Law and the Jewish self-righteousness based on it, cites the multitude of Bible passages which lament over the falling away, unbelief and unrighteousness of the Jewish nation and speaks of the Devils with whom he compares the Jews]

WORSE THAN THE HEATHEN

How much better it would be for them if they did not have God's Commandment or did not know it. For if they did not have it, they would be uncondemned. They are condemned because they have God's Commandment and do not keep it, but act against it without ceasing...

In like manner murderers and whores, thieves and scoundrels and all evil men could boast they are God's holy and chosen people, because they have His Word and know that they should fear and obey Him, love Him and serve Him, honor His Name, do not commit murder, do not commit adultery, etc.... Since, however, they are sinning and are condemned, it is certain that they have the most holy and correct Word of God against which they are sinning. Let them boast, like the Jews, that God has sanctified them through His Law, and chosen them before all people as His peculiar nation.

Such is also the glory of the Jews when they boast in their schools, praise and thank God that He has sanctified them through His Law and made them His chosen nation, while they are well aware that they are keeping none of those things, are filled with pride, envy, usury, avarice and all meanness, and most of all those among them who act very pious and holy in their prayers. For they are so blinded that they do not only practice usury (that I should be silent about their other vices), but teach it as a right which God had commanded them through Moses, in which as in other ways also, they lie about God in a miserable manner, about which there is no time to speak now.

THEY MOCK THE TEN COMMANDMENTS— MAKE OF GOD A FOOL

If the Ten Commandments are not kept, what is the keeping of other commandments otherwise than jugglery and trickery, yea, a real mockery in which God is treated like a fool? Just as if a mean Devilshead among us would march along in robes of bishop or preacher, and keep all the laws and ways of such persons outwardly, but under that spiritual decoration were a real Devil, wolf, an enemy of the Church and a blasphemer who would tread under foot, curse and condemn both the Gospel and the Ten Commandments: 0 what a wonderful saint that would be before God.

Or if in this world a beautiful woman were to parade in a wreath (token of virginity) and follow all manners, rights and behavior of maidenly modesty and virginity, but underneath were nothing but a nasty, shameful whore transgressing the Ten Commandments, what would her fine obedience help her if outwardly she observed the rights and ways of virginity? This it would do to her, that people would despise her seven times more than a free, public whore! Thus God always chided Israel a mean whore through His prophets, because they practiced all manner of idolatry and wickedness under the show of outward commandments and sanctity. As Hosea especially laments Chapter 2:4, 5: *"I will not have mercy upon her children; for they be the children of whoredoms. For their mother hath played the harlot she that conceiveth them hath done shamefully: for she said, I will go after my lovers, that give me my bread and my water, my wool and my flax, mine oil and my drink."* It is nice indeed to find a maiden or woman who is pious, cleanly and decently dressed and outwardly behaving in a modest manner. But when she is a whore, the dress, decorations, wreath and trinkets would appear more honest on a sow in the mire. As Solomon says: *"A golden braid on the nose of a sow is as a beautiful, silly woman."*

Therefore, they might as well keep from boasting about outward obedience to the Laws of Moses without true obedience to God's Ten Commandments. Yea, it makes them sevenfold more unworthy to be the people of God than the heathen.

Let them alone! And let us remain with those who pray the Miserere, the 51st Psalm, that is, who know and understand what the Law is and what is keeping or not keeping the Law.

From this, dear Christian, note what you are doing when you permit these blinded Jews to mislead you. In such an instance the proverb certainly is fulfilled: *"Where the blind leads the blind, both will fall into the ditch."* More you cannot learn from them. To lack understanding of God's commandments and yet be proud and overbearing towards the heathen who are much better than they are before God, because they do not have such pride of holiness, and yet do much more of the Law than the proud saints and condemned blasphemers and liars.

THEIR SCHOOLS A DEVIL'S NEST

Therefore be on your guard against the Jews and know that where they have their schools there is nothing but the Devil's nest in which self-praise, vanity, lies, blasphemy, disgracing God and man, are practiced in the bitterest and most poisonous way as the Devils do themselves. Wherever you see or hear a Jew teaching, do not think otherwise than that you are hearing a poisonous Basiliskus who with his face poisons and kills people. (Medieval legend.) Through God's wrath they have been delivered to believe that all of their boasting, vanity, lying to God, cursing all men, are right and a great service to God, something well becoming to such noble blood of the fathers and circumcised saints (no matter how mean they otherwise might know themselves to be in gross vices) which service they think they have rendered hereby. Look out for them!

They brag and boast that they have had the land of Canaan, the city of Jerusalem and the temple from God. Although God has overthrown such boasting and vanity many times, especially through the king of Babylon who led them away and destroyed everything, like the King of Assyria had before led away and destroyed the entire Israel. Finally they were rooted up and devastated by the Romans, now almost 1400 years ago, that they might comprehend how God did not consider, nor will He regard country, city, temple, priesthood and principality, that He should consider them His own chosen people on that account; yet their iron neck (as Isaiah calls it) is not bowed, nor has their iron forehead become red with shame. They constantly remain stiff-necked, blinded, hardened, and immovable. Still hope that God will bring them home again and give everything back to them.

DEVIL POSSESSED

They do not see and hear that God had given everything for the purpose that they should keep His Commandments: therefore they should be His people and Church. Just as they boast of their blood and nobility, but that they should keep His Commandments, on account of which and for which purpose he had chosen them, that they do not see and regard. They boast about their circumcision, but the purpose for which they were circumcised-- to keep Gods Commandment--does not mean anything to them. They know how to boast of their Law, Temple, Divine Services, city, country and principality; but disregard the purpose for which they had it. The Devil has possessed these people with all his angels; that they always boast of outward things, their gifts, their accomplishments and deeds, which is to offer up the empty shells without the kernels. Those He is to look upon and on their account take them (the people who offer them) for His nation, exalt and bless them above all heathen. But that they should keep His Commandments and keep Him as their God, that they will not accept. The saying of Moses applies to them: *"They do not regard Me as God, therefore I do not regard them as my people,"* as also says Hosea 1:9.

If God had not permitted the people of Jerusalem to be torn asunder and driven them from the land, but had let them keep it after as before, no one could convince them that they are not God's chosen nation. Because they would still have the temple, city and country, regardless of their wickedness. disobedience and stiff-neckedness. Although many prophets would daily cry out and a thousand Moses' be standing here and exclaiming: "You are not the people of God, because you are disobedient and rebellious." Even now they cannot give up their insane raving boast that they are the chosen people of God, after they have been dispersed and rejected for 1500 years! Still they hope to get back there because of their own merits. There is no promise for that on which they could lean for comfort, except what they smear into the Scriptures according to their own imagination...Thus the Jews at last continue in their willfulness, and knowingly want to err and not leave their Rabbis, and therefore we also must leave them to their poisonous blasphemies and lies, and disregard them.

DISHONEST WITH SCRIPTURE

I have also had this experience...Three learned Jews came to me in the hope of finding a new Jew in me, because here in Wittenberg we began to read Hebrew. They also pretended that things would soon improve because we Christians were reading their books. When I disputed with them, they acted according to their kind; gave me their interpretations. When I compelled them to remain with the text, they fell from the text and said they had to believe their Rabbis, as we had to believe the Bishops and Doctors, etc....Then I had mercy on them, gave them a recommendation for safe-conduct to the guides, that they should permit them to pass for the sake of Christ. Later I was informed that they called Christ a "Tola," i.e., a hanged malefactor. Therefore, I do not care to have anything to do with any Jew. St. Paul says they are given over to wrath. The more you try to help them the harder and more wicked they become. Let them alone! [Here follow many proofs from the Bible which are accompanied by detailed theological, scientific, and therefore in general not understood, citations, which cannot be restated here because of their volume, although they are powerful and correspond with Luther's German essence and often strike the nail on the head in a preciously forward manner. From the wealth of striking Scripture passages, only the following are here cited: Haggai 2:6,7: *"Thus saith the Lord of Hosts: yet, once, it is a little while and I will shake the heavens, and the earth, and the sea, and the dry land. And I will shake all nations! and the desire of all nations shall come."* - ("All nations" is equal to "heathen"). Under the "Desire of Nations" the ancient people designated the "Messiah."]

The Jews deny that He came when the temple was still standing and claim that He shall *still* come, as they now have been waiting 1568 years after the destruction of that same temple-- and cannot be called a "little while," because they do not yet know the end of such a "long while."

GOLD AND SILVER THEIR MESSIAH

He will never come, for He has missed the "little while" and has gotten into the great, long while, which will never come to anything. For the prophet speaks of a "little while," not of a great, long while!

But here they squirm out of it in this way: since they cannot deny the "little while," they take the expression: "Desire of Nations," in Hebrew "Hemdath," by itself, and crucify it. Say it should not designate "Messiah," but should denote all gold and silver of the heathen.

Because the word "Hemdath," according to the grammar, really means *"Desire and love for,"* as that which the heathen desire and love. And now the text shall read thus: "After a little while the desire of all heathen shall come." What is that? What do the heathen desire? Gold, silver, and jewels. You may be inclined to ask why the Jews insert such interpretations here. I will say: Their breath stinks for the gold and silver of the heathen, since no people under the sun always have been, still are, and always will remain more avaricious than they (the Jews) as can be noticed in their cursed usury. They also find comfort with this: "When Messiah comes, He shall take all the gold and silver in the world and distribute it among them (the Jews)." Thus wherever they can direct Scripture to their insatiable avarice (desire for money) they wickedly do so. You would think that God and His prophets did not know of anything else to prophecy than how the fathomless avarice of the Jews could be satisfied with the silver and gold of the heathen.

Since childhood they have devoured such poisonous hatred against the Goyim from their parents and Rabbis, and still devour such without ceasing, that according to Psalm 109 it has gone over into their flesh and blood, bone and marrow, and has become their life and being. And as little as they can alter flesh and blood, bone and marrow, so little can they change such pride and envy. They just have to stay that way and be ruined, if God does not perform a special miracle.

A BITTER, POISONOUS ENEMY

Therefore know, my dear Christian, that next to the Devil you have no more bitter, more poisonous, more vehement an enemy than a real Jew who earnestly desires to be a Jew. There may be some among them who believe what the cow or the goose believes. But all of them are surrounded with their blood and circumcision. In history, therefore, they are often accused of poisoning wells, stealing children and mutilating them; as in Trent, Weiszensee, etc. Of course, they deny this. Be it so or not, however, I know full well that the full, ready will is not lacking with them if they could only transform it into deeds, in secret or openly. Know this for a certainty and act accordingly!

Should they at times do something good, however, know full well that it is not done out of love for you, nor for your good. In order to have space to live among us they must of necessity do something. But their heart is and remains as I have said. Do you not want to believe me? Then read Lyra, Burgen and others, honourable and truthful men. If they had not written it, Scripture reveals that the two seeds of the serpent and of the woman are at enmity, and there is no concord between God and the Devil. This is also found in gross form in their writings and prayerbooks.

A person who does not know the Devil, might wonder why they are so at enmity with the Christians above all others; for which they have no reason, since we only do good to them. They live among us in our homes, under our protection, use land and highways, market and streets. Princes and government sit by, snore and have their mugs (mouth) open, let the Jews take from their purse and chest, steal and rob whatever they will. That is, they permit themselves and their subjects to be abused and sucked dry and reduced to beggars with their own money, through the usury of the Jews. For the Jews, as foreigners, certainly should have nothing; and what they have certainly must be ours. They do not work, do not earn anything from us, neither do we donate or give it to them. Yet they have our money and goods and are lords in our land where they are in exile.

If a thief steals ten gulden he must hang; if he robs people on the highway, his head is gone. But a Jew, when he steals ten tons of gold through his usury, is dearer than God Himself.

IN SECRET THEY CURSE US

And as a distinguishing mark, they strengthen their faith and bitter hatred against us by saying among themselves: "Keep on, see how God is with us and does not forsake His people in exile. We do not work, we enjoy good, lazy days; the cursed Goyim must work for us, we get their money; thereby we are their masters, they, however, our servants. Keep on, dear Children of Israel, it will bc better still! Our Messiah will come if we thus continue and appropriate to ourselves, by usury, the "Hemdath" (Hebrew: desire, possessions) of the heathen!"

Well, all this we accept from them while we are protecting them: yet they curse us, as said before. But of this later.

[After lengthy exegetical, historical dissertations there follows a highly interesting paragraph from which it may be seen that Luther was acquainted with the Talmud and Schulchan-Aruch already at this time, which explains his changed attitude over against the Jew question.]

Do not their Talmud and Rabbis write that it is no sin to kill if a Jew kills a heathen, but it is a sin if he kills a brother in Israel! It is no sin if he does not keep his oath to a heathen. Therefore, to steal and rob (as they do with their usury) from a heathen, is a divine service. For they hold that they cannot be too hard on us nor sin against us, because they are the noble blood and circumcised saints; we however, cursed Goyim. And they are the masters of the world and we are their servants, yea, their cattle! In short, as the Rabbis have taught them, so also their Evangelists tell us (Matthew 15:6, *"And honour not his father or his mother, he shall be free. Thus have ye made the Commandment of God of none effect by your tradition."*) that they have abolished the Fifth Commandment about. honouring father and mother; and Matthew 23:13 *("But woe unto you, scribes and Pharisees, hypocrites! for ye shut up the kingdom of heaven against men: for ye neither go in yourselves, neither suffer ye them that are entering to go in."*) practiced more shameful doctrines, not to mention what Christ says, Matthew 5:28: *"But I say unto you, That whosoever looketh on a woman to lust after her hath committed adultery with her already in his heart."* How they cunningly preached and expounded the Ten Commandments! And into the temple they had placed money changers, merchants and all manner of avaricious trade, that our Lord Christ said they had made of God's house a den of thieves. Now figure it out for yourself what a fine honor that was, how the house was full of glory that God had to call his own house a den of thieves! Because so many souls were murdered through avaricious, false doctrine; that is, through two-fold idolatry. To this day the Jews cling to such doctrines and do as their fathers did: pervert the Word of God, are avaricious, practice usury, steal, commit murder (wherever they can do so) and on and on teach their children to do such.

TALMUD WORSE THAN
HEATHEN PHILOSOPHY

The heathen philosophers and poets write much more honourably; not only about Gods government and future life, but also about temporal virtues. They write that man is by nature obligated to serve others, also to keep his word to enemies, and be true and helpful to them especially in need, as taught by Cicero and his like. Yea, I maintain that in three fables of Aesop there is more wisdom to be found than in all the books of the Talmudists and Rabbis and more than ever could come into the hearts of the Jews.

Should someone think I am saying too much--I am not saying too much, but much too little! For I see in writings how they curse us Goyim and wish us all evil in their schools and prayers. They rob us of our money through usury, and wherever they are able, they play us all manner of mean tricks: (what is worst of all) they mean to have right and well in this, that is, they think they have rendered God a service in this and teach that such should be done. No heathen has done such things and none would do so except the Devil himself and those whom he possesses, like he possesses the Jews.

Burgensis, who was a very learned Rabbi among them and by the grace of God became a Christian (which seldom occurs), is much moved that in their schools they so horribly curse us Christians (as Lyra also writes) and from that draws the conclusion that they must not be the people of God. For if they were the people of God, they would act like the captive Jews did in Babylon, to whom Jeremiah writes thus: *"Pray for the King of the city where you are captive; for their peace is also your peace."* But our bastards and false Jews think they must curse us, hate and do us all manner of harm wherever they can do so; for which they have no reason whatsoever. Therefore they certainly are not God's people. More about this later.

THEY PROFANE THE NAME OF JESUS

[Very interesting are the dissertations about the sophisticated manner of the Jews in hiding their hatred against Jesus under sham names. I Here it says:]

Accordingly they treat His (Jesus') Name. For Jhesus in Hebrew means "Healer" or "Helper." The ancient Saxons used a name "Helprich" or "Hilprich," which sounds like the name Jhesus which we now would call "Helprich," that is, who may or should be able to help. Distortingly, however, the Jews call Him "Jesu," which in Hebrew is neither name nor word, but simply three letters or ciphers, or cipherletters, as if I were to take the letters CLU as ciphers and make the word CLU out of them, that is 155 (CLU, Roman ciphers: C -100, L-50, V -5--155. V and U originally are the same). Thus they call Jesu, that is 316. Such a figure is said to bring about another word which means Nebel Borik. About this you may read more in Anton, Margaritham. What Devil's work they practice with such numbers and words.

They treat us Christians in like manner. When we come to them and they receive us they pervert the word: God welcome you (German— seid Gott wilkommen) and say: "Shed wil kom." that is: "Devil, come!" or "There comes a Devil." Since we do not understand the Hebrew, they secretly practice their hatred against us, that we think they are friendly to us while they curse us with the fire of hell and all misfortune.

THEY CALL THE VIRGIN MARY A WHORE

Thus they call Him (Jesus) the child of a whore and His mother, Mary, a whore, whom she had in adultery with a smith. Reluctantly I must speak so coarse in opposing the Devil. Now they well know that they speak such lies in plain hatred and wilfulness, solely to poison their poor youth and simple Jews against the Person of our

Lord, to prevent them from accepting His doctrine (which they cannot deny). Sabastianus Muenster also points out in his Biblia, that there is said to be a poisonous Rabbi who does not call the dear mother "Maria," but "Haria," a heap of mud. And who knows what more they have among themselves of which we know nothing!

[Luther now shows in elaborate, scientific discussions about the Messiah and Bar Kochab, his thorough knowledge of the Jewish character, the writings and hopes of Juda and finally arrives at the so-called "captivity" among the Christians.]

Now behold what a nice thick, fat lie it is when they complain about being captives among us. Jerusalem was destroyed more than 1400 years ago and during that time we Christians have been tortured and persecuted by the Jews in all the world. For nearly 300 years (as stated above) we might well complain that during the time they captured and killed the Christians, which is the clear truth. On top of that, we do not know to this day which Devil brought them into our country. We did not fetch them from Jerusalem!

On top of all that, no one is holding them now. Land and highways are open to them; they may move to their country whenever they care to do so! We would like to add a present in order to get rid of them. They are a heavy burden to us in our country, like a plague, pestilence, and nothing but misfortune.

Do you call that being held captive when a person cannot stand one in his own house? Why, they hold us Christians in captivity in our own country; they let us work in the sweat of our noses, while they appropriate money and goods, sitting behind the stove, are lazy, gluttlers and guzzlers, live well and easy on goods for which we have worked, keep us and our goods in captivity through their cursed usury, mock us and spit on us, because we must labor and permit them to be noblemen at our expense; thus they are our lords and masters, we their servants with our own property, sweat and labor! And to thank us and reward us, they curse our Lord!

ENSLAVE US WITH OUR OWN WEALTH

Should the Devil not laugh and dance, when in this manner he can have his paradise among us Christians, that through the Jews, his saints, he devours what is ours and to thank us fills our mugs (mouths) and noses, blasphemes and curses God and man!

They could not have enjoyed such good days in Jerusalem under David and Solomon in their own possessions as they now have in our property, which

35

they daily steal and rob. Still they complain that we are holding them captive! Yes, we have and hold them captive, as I would like to keep my rheumatism, furuncles and all other diseases and misfortune, who must wait as a poor servant, with money and property and everything I have! I wish they were in Jerusalem with the Jews and whomsoever they would like to have with them!

Since it is certain that we do not hold them captive, how do we deserve that such great and noble saints are so angry with us? We do not call our wives whores as they call Maria, the Mother of Jesus; we do not call them bastards, as they call our Lord Christ. We do not curse them, but wish them all manner of bodily and spiritual good, permit them to lodge with us. We don't steal and mutilate their children; do not poison their water; do not thirst after their blood. With what do we deserve such terrible wrath and envy and hatred of such holy children of God?

It is not otherwise than we have quoted from Moses, that God has struck them with insane blindness and a raving heart, thus it is our fault that we do not avenge the innocent blood which they shed on our Lord, and the Christians, for three hundred years after the destruction of Jerusalem, and from that time on children (which still shines from their eyes and skin). That we do not slay them, but for all their murder, cursing, blaspheming, and disgracing, permit them to dwell among us without charge, protect their schools, houses, body and goods, by which we make them lazy and secure and help them confidently to squeeze from us our money and goods, and in addition to mock us and spit on us, hoping finally to overcome us and slay all of us for such great sin and take away all of our goods, as they daily pray for.

Now tell me, do they not have great cause to hate us cursed Goyim, to curse us and seek our final, thorough and eternal ruin?

Now what are we going to do with these rejected, condemned, Jewish people?

We should not suffer it after they are among us and we know about such lying, blaspheming and cursing among them, lest we become partakers of their lies, cursing, and blaspheming. We cannot extinguish the unquenchable fire of God's wrath (as the prophets say), nor convert the Jews. We must practice great mercy with prayer and godliness that we might rescue a few from the flame and violent heat.

We are not permitted to take revenge. Revenge is around their neck a thousand times greater than we could wish them. I will give you my true counsel: **First**, that we avoid their synagogues and schools and warn people against them. And such should be done to the glory of God and Christendom, that God may see that we are Christians and have not knowingly tolerated such lying, cursing and blaspheming of His Son and His Christians. For what we so far have tolerated in ignorance (I myself did not know it, however, and in spite should before our very noses tolerate such a building for the Jew in which they blaspheme, curse, spit upon and disgrace Christ and us, that would be simply too much, as if we did it ourselves and much worse, as you well know. Moses writes in Deuteronomy that where a city practiced idolatry, it should be entirely destroyed with fire and leave nothing. If he were living today he would be the first to put fire to the Jew schools and houses. [Followed by proofs from Scripture.]

Secondly, that you also refuse to let them own houses among us. For they practice the same thing in their houses as they do in their schools. Instead, you might place them under a roof, or stable, like the Gypsies, to let them know that they are not lords in our country as they boast, but in exile as captives, like without ceasing they howl bloody murder and complain about us before God.

Thirdly, that you take away from them all of their prayer books and Talmuds wherein such lying, cursing, and blaspheming is taught.

Fourthly, that you prohibit their Rabbis to teach. For they have forfeited the right to such an office, because they keep the poor Jews captive with the passage of Moses 7:11, 12, who there commands them to obey their teachers under threat of losing body and soul. Moses clearly adds, "What they teach you according to the law of the Lord." This the profligates pass over, and use the obedience of the poor people for their own wilfulness against the law of the Lord, and pour out for them such poison and blasphemy.

Fifthly, that protection for Jews on highways be revoked. For they have no right to be in the land, because they are not lords, nor officials. They should stay at home I am told that at this time a wealthy Jew is riding with twelve horses in our country. He wants to become a Kochab. [Star Bar-Kochba, "Star Son," false Messiah, was leader of the last rebellion of the Jews against the Romans 132/5 after Christ.]

He practices his usury on princes and lords, land and people. High officials close an eye to it. If you princes and masters do not forbid land and highways to such usurers, I would like to assemble a cavalry against you, because you will learn from this book what the Jews are and how they are to be treated and their activities not to be protected. For you should not and cannot protect them unless you want to be partners of their abominations. What good would be the result, you may well consider and perish.

Sixthly, that their usury be prohibited, which was prohibited by Moses, where they are not lords in their own country over strange lands, and take away all the currency and silver and gold and put it away for safekeeping. For this reason, everything they have they have stolen from us (as said above) and robbed through their usury, since they have no other income. Such money should he used as follows: whenever a Jew is truly converted, he be given one, two, or three hundred flo (measure of money) according to his person, that he may begin to support his poor wife and child and/or support the aged and infirm. For such property which was obtained dishonestly is cursed where it is not turned to good use with God's blessing.

THEY EVEN BETRAYED MOSES

Whenever they boast that Moses had permitted them to practice usury against strangers. (Deuteronomy 23:20, *"Unto a stranger thou mayest lend upon usury; but unto thy brother thou shalt not lend upon usury: that the Lord thy God may bless thee in all that thou settest thine hand to in the land whither thou goest to possess it."*) Otherwise they have not one letter in their favor- they are to be given the following answer: There are two kinds of Jews or Israel. The First are those whom Moses led out of Egypt into the land of Canaan, as God had commanded him; to them he gave *His law,* which they were to keep *in that land, not beyond;* and that only until Messiah should come... The other are the Kaiser's (Caesar's) Jews, not Moses' Jews. They had their origin at the time of the governor Pilate in the land of *Juda*. For when he asked them before his tribunal, "What shall I do with Jesus who is called the Christ?" They cried: "Crucify Him, crucify Him!" He said: "Shall I crucify your king?" They cried out: "We have no king but Caesar (Kaiser)." Such obedience to Caesar, God had not commanded them, they did this on their own accord. Thereupon when Caesar demanded obedience, they resisted and rebelled against him, did not want to be Caesar's now. Then he came and visited his subjects, took them away from Jerusalem and dispersed them throughout his entire domain where they had to be obedient.

Of such are the present remaining dregs of the Jews, of whom Moses knows nothing; they also know nothing of him, for they do not keep one passage in Moses. They must first come back into the land of Canaan and become Moses' Jews, keep his commandment, subdue heathen and strangers under themselves. There they may practice usury as much as the strangers will stand for.

Since, however, they are disobedient to Moses in a strange land under the Kaiser, they should keep the Kaiser's law and not practice usury against their superiors until they become obedient to Moses. For the land which they should possess on the other side of Canaan or the nation of Israel. For he was not sent to Egyptians, Babylonians, or any other nation, with his law, but solely and alone to that nation which he brought out of the land of Egypt into the land of Canaan, as he himself often states in Deuteronomy: They should keep such commandments in the land which they should possess on the other side of the river Jordan.

Inasfar as priesthood, ceremonies, principality, which were mostly built by Moses, have fallen, now almost 1400 years ago, it is certain that his law, which was in existence before that time, also has fallen and come to an end. Therefore the Kaiser's Jews should be treated according to the Kaiser's law and not be treated like Moses' Jews of whom for 1400 years none have existed. For they have no land of their own, much less strange land, where they might practice usury according to Moses.

Finally: That young, strong Jews be given flail, ax, spade, spindle, and let them earn their bread in the sweat of their noses as imposed upon Adam's children, Genesis 3:19-- *"In the sweat of thy face shalt thou eat bread, till thou return unto the ground; for out of it wast thou taken: for dust thou art, and unto dust shalt thou return."* For it will not do that they should let us cursed Goyim work in the sweat of our brow, while they, the

42

holy people, devour our bread in laziness behind the stove and then boast that they are masters over the Christians; but their laziness should be driven from their back.

Should we be concerned, however, that they might do bodily harm to us, to wife and children, servants, cattle, etc., when they serve us or should be compelled to work, because it is to be surmised that such noble lords of the world and poisonous, bitter worms, who are not accustomed to work, would be very remiss to humble themselves under the cursed Goyim; let us apply the ordinary wisdom of other nations like France, Spain, Bohemia, et al., who made them give an account of what they had taken from them by usury and divided it evenly; but expelled them from their country. For, as heard before, God's wrath is so great over them that through soft mercy they only become more wicked, through hard treatment, however, only a little better. Therefore, away with them!

CHARITABLE WITH OUR WEALTH

I hear it said that the Jews give large sums of money and thereby are helpful to the government. Yes, from what do they give it? Not of their own, but from the property of the rulers and subjects, whom they deprive of their possessions through usury! And thus the rulers take from the subjects what the Jews have taken, that is: subjects must give money and suffer themselves to be fleeced for the Jews so they can remain in the land freely to lie, slander, curse and steal. Should not the despairing Jews have a good laugh over the way we suffer ourselves to be fooled and be led around by the nose to give our money in order that they may stay in the land to practice all manner of wickedness? On top of all that they even become rich on our sweat and blood, but we become poor and are sucked dry by them? If that is right, that a servant, yea, a guest, or a captive may annually give to his host ten flo, and in return steal a thousand, the servant and guest will soon be rich, and the master and host in a short time a beggar. Even if the Jews could give the government such sums from their own, which is not possible, and thereby purchase from us protection openly to lie about, slander, spit upon, and curse our Lord Christ in their schools; and wish on us all manner of misfortune, that all of us be stabbed and perish with our Haman, Kaiser, Princes, Lords, wife and children, that certainly would mean for Christ our Lord, the entire Christendom together with our principality, our wives, and children, to be sold miserably cheap.

The traitor Judas would be valued a much greater saint than we. Yea, if every Jew could annually give 100,000 flo; yet we should not permit them to have power to blaspheme, curse, spit upon one single Christian and practice their usury on him. That would be selling ourselves much too cheap. How much more unbearable is it that we should permit the entire Christendom and all of us to be bought with our own money, be slandered and cursed by the Jews who on top of all that he made rich, and our lords, who would laugh us to scorn and be tickled by their audacity!

What a joyful affair that would be for the Devil and his angels and cause them to laugh through their noses like a sow grinning at her little pigs, but deserving real wrath before God.

ADVICE TO RULERS

To sum up, dear princes and lords who have Jews under themselves: if my advice is not acceptable, you may find a better one, that all of us be relieved of the unbearable, devilish burden of the Jews and not become partakers before God of all the lies, slander, spitting, cursing of the raving Jews against the person of our Lord Jesus Christ, His mother, all Christians, all rulers and ourselves, as they freely and deliberately practice it. That you do not let them have protection or safe-conduct, nor fellowship. Neither permit your money and goods, and the money and goods of your subjects, to serve the Jews through their usury. We still have plenty of our own sins and daily add much to them through our ingratitude and despising God's grace and work; that it is not necessary to add to them these mean foreign vices of the Jews and also give them our money and goods. Let us remember that we are daily fighting against the Turk and therefore are much in need of getting rid of our own sins and of spiritual growth and improvement. With this I want to have my conscience cleared and excused as one who has truly exposed the danger and warned against it.

And you, my dear sirs and friends, who are pastors and preachers: I hereby wish to have dutifully reminded of your office, that you also warn your parishioners against their eternal ruin, as you well know how to do; namely, that they be on their guard against the Jews and avoid them. Not that they should curse them and inflict personal harm! For they have cursed and insulted themselves too much by cursing the Man Jesus of Nazareth, Mary's son, as unfortunately they have been doing for 1400 years. In this respect you may let the government deal with them as I have said. Whether or not the government does anything about it, every individual should take care of himself and his conscience, by keeping before himself such a definition or picture of a Jew!

DESIRE THE DEATH OF THE CHRISTIANS

Whenever you see or think about a Jew, say to yourself as follows: Behold, the mouth which I see there has every Saturday cursed, execrated, and spit upon my dear Lord, Jesus Christ who has redeemed me with His precious blood; and also prayed and cursed before God that I, my wife and children, and all Christians should be stabbed and perish in the most miserable manner -would like to do so himself if he could be that he might come into possession of our goods.

Perhaps he has this very day often spit on the ground over the Name of Jhesu (according to their custom) and that the spittle is still clinging to his mouth and beard where there is still room for it. Should I eat, drink with, or speak to such a Devilish mug (mouth)? I might devour many Devils, as for a certainty I would become partaker of all the Devils who live in that Jew, and would spit upon the precious blood of Christ, God keep me from doing that!

If they do not believe as we do, we cannot help it and cannot compel anyone to accept the faith. We, however, should avoid strengthening them in their deliberate lying, blaspheming, cursing and disagreeing, also do not become partakers of their devilish raving and ranting by

47

according them protection, meat and drink, lodging and other neighborly kindness. Especially because they proudly and haughtily boast, wherever we are friendly to them or serve them, that God has made them to be lords and us to be servants. As when a Christian on the Sabbath lights their fire and cooks for them whatever they desire, for which they curse, bespit and slander us as if they were doing something good, and yet eat up our goods which they have stolen from us. Such a despairing, evil, poisonous thing it is with these Jews who these 1400 years have been and still are our plague, pestilence and all misfortune.

ADVICE TO PREACHERS

Especially you who are preachers: where there are Jews, diligently insist that your masters and regents remember the duties of their office as they owe it to God, and compel the Jews to work, forbid them to practice usury and stay their blaspheming and cursing. For if they punish thieves, robbers, murderers, slanderers and other vices among us Christians, why should the Devil's children among the Jew be free to do such things against us? Do we not suffer more from them than the Wals from the Spaniards? They take from their host; kitchen, cellar, chest, money bag, and in addition curse them and threaten them with death. In like manner we are treated by the Jews, our guests; we are the hosts. Thus they rob and deprive us, recline on our neck, the lazy and idle bellies, are gluttons in eating and drinking, have easy days in our homes and as a reward curse our Lord Christ, Church, princes and all of us without ceasing to threaten us and to wish us death and all misfortune. Just think, how do we poor Christians get that way that we enrich such idle people, such blaspheming enemies of God and receive nothing in return but their cursing, slandering and all misfortune that they can do and wish against us? In this respect we are blind dogs, such as the Jews are in their unbelief; that we suffer such tyranny from such merciless knaves, do not see and feel such, to let them be our lords, yea, our raving tyrants. We are, however, their captives and subjects; and still they lament that we are holding them as captives, mock us on top of all that as if we had to accept it from them! If the rulers, however, refuse to compel them nor restrain their devilish wantonness, that they be driven from the country, as said, and be told that they move to their own land and possessions in Jerusalem and there lie, curse, blaspheme, spit, murder, steal, rob, practice usury, mock, and engage in all such slanderous abominations as they do among us; and leave us our land, principality, body, goods, much more, our Lord Jesus, faith and church undisturbed and unbesmirched with such devilish tyrannies and wickedness. Of course, they could pretend that this would not help them. For no one has the right to grant liberty to practice such abominations, and all liberties are thereby lost.

After you pastors and preachers have diligently and dutifully issued such warning, and neither master nor subjects will do anything about it, then let us (as Christ says) shake the dust from our shoes and say: we are innocent of your blood. For I can see and have often had the experience how lenient and merciful the reversed world is; where it should be stern, and again is stern where it should be lenient and merciful. The Prince of this world rules like King Ahab, II Kings, 20. In like manner they may not want to be lenient with the Jews, these blood-thirsty enemies of our Christian and human name, to earn heaven therewith. But for the Jews to hold in captivity, plague, torture and inflict all misery on us poor Christians with all such devilish cruelties as described above,-- that we should suffer and is considered a good, Christian indeed, especially where there is money which they have stolen from us.

What are we poor preachers to do meanwhile?

First, we want to believe that our Lord Jesus is truthful when He says of such Jews who do not accept Him, but crucified Him: "*You are vipers* *and children of the Devil.*" As His forerunner, John the Baptist also says. Now such rulers and such merciful saints who wish the Jews well, will be the last to let us alone to believe in our Lord Jesus Christ, who, of course, knows all hearts better than such merciful saints; that these Jews must be a generation of vipers and children of the Devil; that is, who grant us just as much good as their father, the Devil. What good that fellow has done to us, we Christians should have understood long and well from experience besides the statements of Scripture.

Whoever has a desire to lodge, nurse, and honor such poisonous serpents and young Devils; that is, the worst enemies of Christ our Lord and of us all; and permit himself to be abused, plundered, robbed, spit upon, cursed and suffer all evil, let the Jews be commended to him. If this be not sufficient, let him also be put into his mug or crawl and worship such a sanctuary, and afterward boast that he had been merciful, had strengthened the Devil and his young Devils to blaspheme our dear Lord and the precious blood with which He has bought us. In that way he will be a perfect Christian, filled with deeds of mercy, for which Christ will reward him on Judgment Day with the Jews and eternal hell fire!

If that be rudely spoken it is said to the rude cursing of the Jews! Of which others write much, which also the Jews well understand that it is called cursing, as they who thereby knowingly want to curse and blaspheme.

Let us also speak of this in a subtle, and as Christians, in a spiritual way. Thus says our Lord Jesus Christ: *"Whosoever receiveth Me, receiveth Him that sent Me."* Matthew 10:40; *"He that despiseth you, despiseth Me; and he that despiseth Me, despiseth Him that sent Me."* Luke 10:16; *"He that hateth Me, hateth also my Father."*—John 15:23; *"That all men should honor the Son as they honor the Father. He that honoreth not the Son, honoreth not the Father who hath sent Him."* John 5:23

THEY BLASPHEME THE NEW TESTAMENT

Will you say: Yes, the Jews do not believe and do not know this, because they do not accept the New Testament? I answer: May the Jews know or believe this or that; we Christians know that they openly blaspheme God the Father when they blaspheme and curse this Jesus.

If God would say to us now or on the Day of Judgment: Do you hear, you are a Christian and know that the Jews openly blasphemed and cursed Me and My Son, and you gave them a place to do so, also protected and guarded them so they could do so unhindered and unpunished in your country, city or house! Tell me: What shall we answer?

[Now follow long dissertations, supported by passages from Scripture about the Messianic office of Jesus, which are not given here because of their scientific, theological nature. Finally Luther sums up his presentations as follows:]

Accordingly, we should not joke about this matter, but very sincerely find counsel against it and save our souls from the Jews; that is, from eternal death. As stated before, this counsel is in the first place: that we refuse them the right to have synagogues, so the world may know that we do not permit a house to remain in which the Jews have for so long a time blasphemed our dear Creator and Father, together with His Son, which so far we had tolerated in ignorance.

Secondly: That all of their books be taken away; prayer books, Talmuds, and not one page of it be left; and keep them for those who will become converted. For they use all of that only to blaspheme the Son of God; that is, God Himself, the Father, Creator of heaven and earth, and will never use it in any other way.

Thirdly: That among us and in our possessions they be forbidden openly to praise and thank

God, to pray and to teach. Let them do that in their own country or wherever we Christians do not hear or know about it. The reason for this: their praise, thanks, prayers, and teachings are nothing but blasphemy, cursing, idolatry; since their heart and mouth call God Father Nebel Borik, the same as they call His Son, our Lord Jesus Christ. For as they call and honor the Son, so the Father is likewise called and honored. It will not help them to employ many beautiful words and gloriously use the Name of God. For it is written *"Thou shalt not take the Name of the Lord, thy God, in vain.."* Just as it did not help their forefathers to use the Name of God and still call Him Baal in the time of the kings of Israel.

Fourthly: That they be forbidden to mention the Name of God before our ears, for we cannot suffer that with a clear conscience. When their blasphemous mouth and heart call the Son of God Nebel Borik, they are also calling the Father by the same name; as we Christians cannot understand it otherwise. We must believe that as the Son is named or believed to be, even so the Father is named and believed to be. Therefore the mouth of the Jews should not be considered worthy to mention the Name of God before our ears; but whosoever hear it mentioned by the Jews should Report it to the rulers, etc. And let no one be merciful and kind in this respect; for it concerns the honor of God and the salvation of us all (also of the Jews).

And should they or anyone else propose that they did not mean it so wickedly, neither knew that with such blasphemy and cursing they were blaspheming and cursing God the Father; for they most highly and beautifully praise and honor God, although they slander Jesus and us Christians. That has been answered above as you heard. If the Jews do not want to know it or consider it good, we Christians must know it. So the Jews are not excused because of their ignorance, since God has caused this to be preached for almost 1500 years so that they are obligated to know this and God also requires it of them.

For whosoever hears God's Word for 1500 years and always says: I do not want to know it! The ignorance of such a one will earn him a mean excuse, that is, a sevenfold debt.

THEIR MESSIAH IS FALSE

Lastly will I say this for myself: If God would not want to give me a Messiah who is different from the one the Jews desire and hope for, I would much rather be a sow than a human being! And I will give you some good reasons for this: The Jews desire no more from their Messiah than that He should be a Kochab and a worldly king, who would slay the Christians. divide the world among the Jews and make them rich lords, and finally die like other kings and his children after him likewise.

Of what good would the Jewish Messiah be to me, if he could not help me, poor human being, against my spiritual loss, and could not make my Life one tenth part as good as that of a sow? I would say: Dear Lord God, keep your Messiah or give Him to anyone who will have Him. Me, however, change to a sow, for it is better to be a living sow than an eternally dying human being. Yea, as Christ says: *"It were better for that man if he had never been born!"*

If, however, I had a Messiah who could help me in spiritual need; that I would not have to fear death, would always and eternally be certain of life, could mock at the Devil and hell and would not have to shiver before the wrath of God, then my heart would skip for joy and be drunken with happiness. Then I would light a fire of love for God and never cease to thank and praise Him. If then He would not give me silver and gold and other riches, still the whole world would be a paradise to me even if I should have to live in a prison.

Such a Messiah we Christians have, and for it we thank God the Father with full, overwhelming joy of our hearts! Such a Messiah the Jews do not desire, and of what good would He be to them? They must have one from an earthly Utopia who would satisfy their stinking belly and die with them like a cow or a dog.

BEWARE OF THEIR BLASPHEMY AND USURY

In my opinion it will have to come to this: if we are to stay clean of the Jew's blaspheming and not become partakers of it, we must separate and they must leave our country. Thus they could no more cry and lie to God that we are holding them captive; and we could no more complain that they plague us with their blaspheming and usury. This is the nearest and best advice that makes it safe for both parties.

[Here follow longer proofs from Scripture against the accusation of the Jews against the Christian doctrine.]

So much writing, good Sir and dear Friend, you have compelled me to do about your booklet in which a Jew exhibits his cunning arguments against an absent Christian. Thank God, he would not do so to me at the present time. I hope that in this booklet a Christian who does not desire to become Jewish will find sufficient arguments to guard against the blind, poisonous Jews, and will also become an enemy of the wickedness, lies, and cursing of the Jews, and come to the knowledge that their belief is not only false, but that they are also possessed of all the Devils.

Christ, our dear Lord, graciously convert

them and keep us in the knowledge of Him, which is eternal life, most certainly. AMEN.

Following are paragraphs taken from various sermons and writings of Dr. Luther. After each paragraph the original source of the quotation is indicated.

Note: Quotations from Luther's works marked *"W"* originate from the Weimar Edition, those marked "E" from the Erlangen Edition.

An Appraisal of Mankind

Jews are young devils condemned to Hell. (E. 32, p. 276)

Maybe mild-hearted and gentle Christians will believe I am too rigorous and drastic against the poor, afflicted Jews, believing that I ridicule them and treat them with much sarcasm. By my word, I am far too weak to be able to ridicule such a satanic breed. I would fain do so, but they are far greater adepts at mockery than I and possess a God who is a master in this art; it is the Evil One himself. (E. 32, p. 286)

Even with no further evidence than the Old Testament, I would maintain, and no person on earth could alter my opinion, that the Jews, as they are today, are veritably a mixture of all the depraved and malevolent knaves of the whole world over, who have then been dispersed in all countries, similarly to the Tartars, Gypsies and such folk, to afflict the different nations with their usury, to spy upon others and to betray, to poison wells, to deceive and to kidnap children- in short, to practice all kinds of dishonesty and injury. (Extract from the Phamphlet "Von Schem Hamphoras und vom Geschlecht Christi." 1543.)

The Jewish Danger

Those Jews professing to be surgeons or doctors deprive the Christians who make use of their medicaments, of health and prosperity, for such Jewish doctors believe they find especial favour with their God if they torment and furtively kill Christians. And we, fools that we are, even turn for succor to our enemies and their evil ways in the times when our lives are in danger, which is indeed sorely trying God's patience. (F. 62, p. 367)

Luther's Legacy

As soon as my principal business* has been accomplished, I shall have to devote myself to the expulsion of the Jews. Count Albrecht is hostile towards them and he has already abandoned them, but as yet they are being molested by none. With the help of God I shall, in the sermons I hold from the pulpit, assist Count Albrecht and shall also abandon them. (Extract from one of Luther's letters to his wife, shortly before his death.)

Luther's last Sermon:
"Wanting Against the Jews"**

Besides, you also have many Jews living in the country, who do much harm...You should know that the Jews blaspheme and violate the name of our Saviour day for day...for that reason you, Milords and men of authority, should not tolerate but expel them. They are our public enemies and incessantly blaspheme our Lord Jesus Christ, they call our Blessed Virgin Mary a harlot and her Holy Son a bastard and to us they give the epithet of changelings and abortions. If they could kill us all, they would gladly do so; in fact, many of them murder Christians, especially those professing to be surgeons and doctors. They know how to deal with medicaments in the manner of the Italians—the Borgias and Medicis—who gave people poison which brought about their death in one hour or in a month.

Therefore deal with them harshly as they do nothing but excruciatingly blaspheme our Lord Jesus Christ, trying to rob us of our lives, our health, our honour and belongings...For that reason I cannot have patience nor carry on an intercourse with these deliberate blasphemers and violators of our Beloved Saviour.

As a good patriot I wanted to give you this

warning for the very last time to deter you from participating in alien sins. You must know I only desire the best for you all, rulers and subjects. (E. 62, p. 189)

*The divergencies between the Counts of Mansfeld which were the cause of his journey.

**Held at Eisleben, a few days before his death, February, 1546.

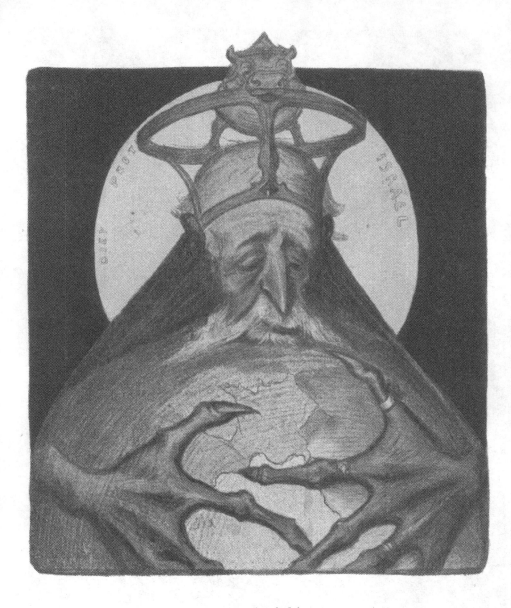

Rothschild

Französische Karikatur von C. Léandre. 1898

7. u. 8. Satiren auf die Juden
Chorstuhlschnitzereien in der Kirche Notre Dame
von Aerschot. 15. Jahrhundert

6. Das Judenschwein am Regensburger Dom

Kapitellverzierung.   Satirische Steinskulptur.   13. Jahrhundert

n   ach dem vñ iüdisch listikeyt
yr fursetzt gar on all arbeyt
mit gätzer faulkeit sich zu nern

14. Bauer und Städter beim jüdischen
Geldverleiher

Nürnberger Holzschnitt 1491

Der Judenspieß bin ich
genant/
Jch far daher durch alle Lande/
Von grossen Juden ich sagen wil
Die schad dem Land thün in der still.
Der Geistlich fellt vnd würt zu nicht
Der weltlich mechtig hoch auff bricht/
Vnd w'andern vmbher in dem Land
Vnser wahr ist laster/sünd vnd schand.

13. Titelholzschnitt der satirischen Schrift: „Der Judenspieß".
Straßburg 1541

16. Die Judensau
Wittenberger Spottbild. Holzschnitt. 16. Jahrhundert

2

Das große Judenschwein

Deutsche Karikatur auf (e Juden. 15. Jahrhun

68

rhundert

Der Jůden Er=
barkeit.

ALhie siehstu der Jüden Tantz/
Ir Gottes Lestrung vnd Finantz/
Wie sie den Son Gotts verspeyen/
All Christen vermaledeyen.
Darzu all Christlich Oberkeit/
Weils nicht gerhet so ists jn leid.
Auch jr grewliche Wucherey/
Noch sind sie bey alln Herren frey.
Betracht doch solchs du fromer Christ/
Du seyst gleich hoch / odr wer du bist.
Las dir dis Buch zu hertzen gan/
Gott wird eim jeden gebn sein lohn.

ANNO. M. D. LXXI.

20. Titelblatt der satirischen Spottschrift „Der Juden Ehrbarkeit". 1571

70

Printed in the USA
CPSIA information can be obtained
at www.ICGtesting.com
LVHW040512051223
765560LV00003B/536